LIGHTHOUSES

A PHOTOGRAPHIC TOUR

LIGHTHOUSES

CAPTIONS BY
JULIE STETZKO TAFF

BROWNTROUT PUBLISHERS, INC.
SAN FRANCISCO

ISBN: 1-56313-925-1
10 9 8 7 6 5 4 3 2 1
Digit on the right indicates the number of this printing

Library of Congress Cataloging-in-Publication Data
Lighthouses / captions by Julie Stetzko Taff.
       p.   cm.
      ISBN 1-56313-925-1
     1. Lighthouses–North America–Pictorial works.   I. Taff, Julie Stetzko, 1952-
VK1022.L54   1998
387.1'55–dc21
                                      98-27703
                                          CIP

Printed and bound in Italy by Milanostampa

Published by:
BrownTrout Publishers, Inc.
Post Office Box 280070
San Francisco, California 94128-0070 U.S.A.
Toll Free: 800 777 7812
Website: browntrout.com

Lighthouse Photography Credits

Page	Lighthouse	Credit
Cover	Heceta Head	©1998 Kathleen Norris Cook
p. 2/3		©1998 Canada In Stock
5	Pigeon Point	©1998 Tom Algire
6/7	Presque Isle	©1998 Tom Algire
8	Fort Gratiot	©1998 Mark Reinholz
9	Sand Island	©1998 Terry Donnelly
10	Sanibel Island	©1998 Jake Rajs
11	Point Aux Barques	©1998 G. Alan Nelson
12	Two Harbors	©1998 Tom Algire
13	South Manitou	©1998 Terry Donnelly
14	St. Augustine	©1998 James Randklev
15	Assateague Island	©1998 Tom Algire
16/17	Whitefish Point	©1998 Fred Hirschmann
18	Cape Blanco	©1998 Tom Algire
19	Cape Lookout	©1998 George Humphries
20	St. Marks	©1998 Tom Algire
21	Ocracoke	©1998 George Humphries
22	Cape Neddick	©1998 Tom Algire
22	Portland Head	©1998 Lawrence Parent
23	Portland Head	©1998 Paul Rezendes
24/25	Long Beach Bar	©1998 Hardie Truesdale
26	Eagle Harbor	©1998 Tom Algire
27	Rondout	©1998 Hardie Truesdale
27	Cape Hatteras	©1998 Hardie Truesdale
28	Peggy's Cove	©1998 Michael Gadomski
29	Wind Point	©1998 Darryl R. Beers
30	West San Benito Island	©1998 Frank S. Balthis
31	Yaquina Bay	©1998 Erwin C. Nielsen
32	Fairport Harbor	©1998 Carl A. Stimac
33	Grand Traverse	©1998 Larry Knupp
34/35	East Brother Island	©1998 David Sanger
36	Santa Cruz	©1998 Bob Barbour
37	Crisp Point	©1998 Mark Reinholz
37	Old Point Loma	©1998 Tom Algire
38	Sitka	©1998 Frank S. Balthis
38	Point Montara	©1998 Markham Johnson
39	Bodie Island	©1998 Nancy Hoyt Belcher
40	Langara	©1998 Dewitt Jones
41	Pemaquid Point	©1998 Thomas Labash
42/43	Fanad Head	©1998 Farrell Grehan
44	Peggy's Cove	©1998 Nancy Hoyt Belcher
45	Big Sable Point	©1998 Ray Malace
45	West San Benito Island	©1998 Frank S. Balthis
46/47	Portland Head	©1998 Tom Algire
48/49	Grand Haven South Pierhead	©1998 Mark Reinholz
50/51	West Quaddy Head	©1998 Peter Urbanski
52	Highlands	©1998 William H. Johnson
53	Marshall Point	©1998 Eric Wunrow
53	Fond du Lac Range Front	©1998 Daniel Dempster
54	Bodie Island	©1998 William H. Johnson
55	Au Sable Point	©1998 Daniel Dempster
56/57	Trinidad Head	©1998 Kathleen Norris Cook
58	Sherwood Point	©1998 Daniel Dempster
59	Tawas Point	©1998 Mark Reinholz
60	Mendota Light	©1998 Tom Algire
61	Point Wilson	©1998 Dave Schiefelbein
62	Point Cabrillo	©1998 Frank S. Balthis
63	Grosse Point	©1998 Darryl R. Beers
64/65	Barnegat	©1998 Tom Till
66	Holland Harbor South Pierhead	©1998 Daniel Dempster
67	Hunting Island	©1998 Hardie Truesdale
68	Point Judith	©1998 Eric Wunrow
68	South Breakwater Outer	©1998 Tom Algire
69	Crooked River	©1998 Denis Duckett / Sky Shots
70	St. Augustine	©1998 Denis Duckett / Sky Shots
71	Boca Grande Rear Range	©1998 Denis Duckett / Sky Shots
72	Whitefish Point	©1998 Mark Reinholz
73	Cape Florida	©1998 Tom Algire
74	Marblehead	©1998 Larry Knupp
75	Forty Mile Point	©1998 Ian Adams
76	Algoma North Pierhead	©1998 Darryl R. Beers
76	Cheboygan Crib	©1998 Darryl R. Beers
77	Split Rock	©1998 Tom Algire
78/79	Cape Florida	©1998 Denis Duckett / Sky Shots
80	Manitowac Breakwater	©1998 Darryl R. Beers
81	Año Nuevo State Reserve	©1998 Frank S. Balthis
82	Kewaunee Pier	©1998 Darryl R. Beers
83	Nobska Pier	©1998 Eric Wunrow
84	Big Bay Point	©1998 Mark Reinholz
85	Cape Meares	©1998 Frank S. Balthis
86/87	Pigeon Point	©1998 Frank S. Balthis
88/89	Quaco	©1998 Nancy Hoyt Belcher
90	Smalls	©1998 Christopher Nicholson
91	Pigeon Point	©1998 Frank S. Balthis
92	Coquille River	©1998 Wood Sabold
93	Waugoshance Shoal	©1998 Ray Malace
94	San Benito Island	©1998 Frank S. Balthis
95	West San Benito Island	©1998 Frank S. Balthis
96/97	Port Dalhousie Front Range	©1998 Mario Madau / Canada In Stock
98/99	Holland Harbor South Pierhead	©1998 Ray Malace
100	Gibbs Hill	©1998 Robert Holmes
101	Longships	©1998 Christopher Nicholson
102/103	Fort Jefferson	©1998 James Randklev
104/105	Sodus Point	©1998 Eric Wunrow
106	Wolf Rock	©1998 Christopher Nicholson
107	Heceta Head	©1998 Kathleen Norris Cook
108/109	Eagle Harbor	©1998 Michael Whye
110/111	Santa Cruz	©1998 Bob Barbour

"There it loomed up, stark and straight, glaring white and black, and one could see the waves breaking in white splinters like smashed glass upon the rocks."

— Virginia Woolf, *To The Lighthouse*

Pigeon Point Lighthouse

Presque Isle Lighthouse
Erie, Pennsylvania

The square brick 68-foot tower of Presque Isle Lighthouse was first lit in 1873. A two-story brick dwelling is attached. This Lake Erie light, with a focal plane 73 feet above lake level, is now automated.

Sand Island Lighthouse
Sand Island, Mobile Bay, Alabama

Sand Island Lighthouse, marking the approach to the entrance to Mobile Bay, is Alabama's only coastal lighthouse. The first tower, built in 1838, was replaced by a new tower in 1859 which was destroyed by Confederate troops during the Civil War. The lighthouse, lit in 1873, fought a constant battle with beach erosion and deadly storms. Once set on a 400-acre island, the brownstone Sand Island Lighthouse stands alone on an outcrop just slightly larger than its base.

ort Gratiot Lighthouse
rt Huron, Michigan

rt Gratiot Lighthouse is thought to be Michigan's oldest ghthouse, guiding sailors from Lake Huron to the entrance f the St. Clair River. Red brick keeper's quarters and fog-histle house stand beside the red brick tower which has en painted white. Poorly constructed in 1825, the original wer was destroyed by a storm and replaced in 1829 by e 82-foot conical tower. The keeper's quarters and a fog-histle house were completed 14 years later.

Sanibel Island Lighthouse
Gulf Coast of Florida

The 102-foot tall skeleton tower of Sanibel Island Lighthouse illuminates Florida's Gulf Coast between Key West and Egmont Key. Construction of the lighthouse was delayed when the transport ship carrying the building materials sunk off the island's coast. Fortunately, the captain unloaded some of the cargo before the ship went down and a diver recovered all but two brackets to complete construction of the lighthouse in 1884. The station includes two square keeper's dwellings built on piles, several water tanks and work buildings.

Point Aux Barques Lighthous
Port Austin, Michig

Point Aux Barques Lighthouse, rebuilt in 1857, is located o the eastern side of Saginaw Bay. One of the tallest and mo powerful lights on the Great Lakes, this white, 89-fo white brick tower on Lake Huron is now automate

South Manitou Lighthouse
Leland, Michigan

Ships traveling to the Mackinac Stratis navigate the Manitou Passage marked by the South Manitou Lighthouse, built in 1872. The tall 104-foot brick tower, surrounded by cheerfully painted keeper's quarters and outbuildings, are part of the Sleeping Bear Dunes National Lakeshore.

o Harbors Lighthouse
Harbors, Minnesota

ding ships transporting iron ore from Two Harbors ough Lake Superior was the job of the massive red brick ht Station built in 1892. Airport-style beacons replaced fourth order Fresnel lens in 1970. Its 50-foot square er, set into the corner of the keeper's dwelling, was npletely automated in 1981.

Assateague Island Light
Chincoteague, Virginia

The 1833 Assateague Island Lighthouse, built by the lowest bidding contractor, proved too low and too poorly lit to adequately warn ships of the dangerous shoals between Cape Charles, Virginia and Cape Henlopen, Delaware. Construction of a new lighthouse began in 1859 but was interrupted by the Civil War. With all renovation complete in 1867, the light from the 142-foot-tall was visible for nineteen miles. Easily recognizable by its glossy red and white striped bands, the active station is part of the Chincoteague National Wildlife Refuge.

Augustine Lighthouse
Augustine, Florida

rking the entrance to the St. Augustine Harbor on Florida's lf Coast, a 73-foot brick tower was erected in 1824 near the of an early Spanish watchtower. The St. Augustine Light 1e under attack from the Confederates during the Civil War. lit in 1867, the lighthouse was again threatened, this time by erosion. The conical tower, painted with distinctive spiral :k and white bands and topped with a red lantern, was lit for first time in 1874 and stands active today.

Whitefish Point Light
Whitefish Point, Michigan

"Superior, they say,
never gives up her dead
When the gales of November
come early."

"Wreck of the *Edmund Fitzgerald*"
© Moose Music, Inc.

Gale force winds and overpowering waves in Lake Superior where the lake approaches Whitefish Bay have claimed many ships, including the well-known *Edmund Fitzgerald*. The light at Whitefish Point, a steel, 80-foot cylinder supported by steel framework, has been a welcome sight to sailors since 1861. It replaced the original masonry light built in 1848. Automated in 1970, Whitefish Point Light is still active. The Great Shipwreck Museum is now located in the keeper's dwelling.

Cape Blanco Light
Port Orford, Oregon

Oregon's oldest lighthouse, Cape Blanco was put into service in 1870 to warn sailors
of the dangerous waters below the steep white Cape Blanco cliffs. The 59-foot tall
conical brick tower stands high on the deceivingly beautiful cliffs, making it Oregon's
highest light with a focal plane of 245 feet above sea level.

Cape Lookout Lig
Beaufort, North Carol

Cape Lookout was labeled *"Promontorium Tremendum"* (Horrible Headlar
by an early mapmaker because of the dangerous shoals extending out fro
the cape for 10 miles. A light was built in 1812 to guide ships seeking refu
from the stormy seas. This light was reportedly a poor aid to navigatio
resulting in the establishment of a new, taller light in 1859. The diago
black and white checkers were painted on the 150-foot tower in 187

Ocracoke Lighthouse
Ocracoke Island, North Carolina

One of the oldest active lights on the southeast coast, Ocracoke Lighthouse was first built by Henry Dearborn on Shell Castle Island in 1803. Destroyed by lightning in 1818, it was rebuilt in 1823 near Ocracoke, an important shipping village. In 1861, Confederates damaged the lens, although the 76-foot white conical masonry tower survived the Civil War. The new lens, installed in 1864, is now automated with its light 75 feet above water level.

. Marks Light
Marks, Florida

rst commissioned in 1828, the hollow-walled light on the nks of the St. Marks River was poorly constructed and d to be demolished. The 1831 masonry tower, threatened erosion, was replaced in 1840 only to have the base own apart by the Confederates during the Civil War. ebuilt in 1867, the picturesque, 82-foot white conical wer with attached work building stands as one of the dest lighthouses on the Gulf Coast.

Cape Neddick Lighthouse, "The Nubble"
York, Maine

Officially named Cape Neddick Light, this picturesque lighthouse is located on a small island off the coast of Maine known to locals and fisherman as "The Nubble." The sculpted rock formations below the station reveal a portrait gallery to imaginative visitors. The 41-foot tower, keeper's house, and support buildings were built in 1879 on the island's highest point, bringing the light's focal plane to 88 feet above sea level.

Portland Head Lighthouse
South Portland, Maine

Portland Head Lighthouse
South Portland, Maine

Portland Head Lighthouse was built in 1791 under orders from George Washington. Already under construction by the Commonwealth of Massachusetts, Portland Head was the first lighthouse completed by the new federal government after the Revolution. The fieldstone tower and quintessential New England keeper's quarters located at the entrance to Portland Harbor appears essentially the same as it did in 1790.

Long Beach Bar Lighthouse
Greenport, New York

First illuminated in 1870, the Long Beach Bar Lighthouse brings vessels in and out of Peconic Bay from Gardiners Bay. Abandoned in 1947 and destroyed by fire in 1963, it was rebuilt and relit and 1990. Rough seas have since done some damage to the reconstructed lighthouse. East End Seaport and Marine Foundation continues raising funds for further renovation.

Eagle Harbor Lighthouse
Eagle Harbor, Michigan

It was the rich deposits of copper discovered in the 1840s that brought ships in and out of Eagle Harbor located on the Keweenaw Peninsula. Eagle Harbor Lighthouse began operation in 1851. Severe Lake Superior winters weathered away the original buildings, which were replaced by a 44-foot octagonal brick tower and attached one-and-a-half-story dwelling in 1871. This most-loved lighthouse on Lake Superior, in its storybook setting, is now automated and cared for by the Keweenaw Peninsula Historical Society.

Rondout Lighthouse
Kingston, New York

Construction of the Rondout Lighthouse at the confluence of the Hudson River and Rondout Creek began in 1915. The buff-colored, 48-foot brick light tower, with its two-and-a-half-story dwelling, was the third to be built at the mouth of the creek. The light was automated in 1954. A 1984 agreement with the Coast Guard, the Hudson River Preservation Society, the state of New York, the Hudson River Heritage Task Force, and the city of Kingston refurbished the Rondout Lighthouse, which now houses a maritime museum.

Cape Hatteras Lighthouse
Buxton, North Carolina

The first light to be established at Cape Hatteras in 1803 protected ships from the rocky coast known as the "graveyard of the Atlantic." The strong currents of the Gulf Stream could send ships crashing over the Diamond Shoals. Navy officers complained of the light's inadequacies, calling it "the worst light in the world." The tower was raised to 150 feet and given a first order Fresnel lens. By the end of the Civil War, Cape Hatteras needed a new tower. Standing 208 feet tall with distinctive black and white spirals, Cape Hatteras, built in 1870, is the tallest brick lighthouse in the United States. Erosion has threatened the tower since the 1930s. The National Park Service targets a 1999 moving date for the landmark station.

Wind Point Lighthouse
Racine, Wisconsin

The Wind Point Lighthouse, completed in 1880, guided ships heading southbound into Racine Harbor with a pair of lenses fitted atop the 108-foot-tall white conical brick tower. A short passageway connects the tower to a one-and-one-half-story keeper's quarters. A fog signal was added in 1900. Budget cuts have forced the Coast Guard to turn many stations over to local governments or non-profit organizations. The Village of Wind Point now maintains this historic site.

eggy's Cove Lighthouse
ova Scotia, Canada

·ggy's Cove is one of the best known, most popular ;hthouses of Canada. The original Peggy's Cove Light-ouse was built in 1868. The present concrete tower, built 1914, is located just a few feet above the site of the old ooden structure which deteriorated and was destroyed.

Shipwreck through lighthouse window, Baja California

Yaquina Bay Lighthou
Newport, Oreg
Only in service for three years due to construction in 1874 of the Yaquina Head Ligh
house only a few miles away, the Yaquina Bay Lighthouse was rescued from demoliti
by local citizens in 1946. The state restored the unique wooden building in 197

Grand Traverse Lighthouse
North Port, Michigan

Located on Cat Head Point, the Grand Traverse Lighthouse has welcomed ships into Grand Traverse Bay from Lake Michigan since 1853. Perched atop the comfortable two-story yellow brick keeper's dwelling is a square tower and lantern room with a fourth order lens. Decommissioned and abandoned in 1972, the lighthouse has since been restored and maintained by the Grand Traverse Lighthouse Foundation.

irport Harbor Lighthouse
rport, Ohio

dway between Ashtabula and Cleveland lies Fairport Harbor where in 1825 on
east side of the Grand River, the original 30-foot tall brick Fairport Harbor
ghthouse was built. Restored in 1941 as a marine museum, the comfortable
o-story keeper's house is reportedly inhabited by the spirit of a small gray kitten.

East Brother Island Lighthouse
Richmond, California

Built 1873–1874 after many land negotiation delays, the East Brother Island Lighthouse shines from East Brother Island in the San Francisco Bay. The Victorian-styled square lighthouse and attached keeper's dwelling which once housed four keepers and an albino frog, is now a bed-and-breakfast inn.

Santa Cruz Light
Lighthouse Point, Santa Cruz, California
The Santa Cruz Light was rebuilt in 1967. As early as 1869 this brick lighthouse stood at the entrance to Santa Cruz Harbor. It is now the home of a surfing museum and a popular attraction of the Santa Cruz Lighthouse Park.

Crisp Point Lighthouse
Vermillion, Michigan

Only the tower and attached small building at Crisp Point remain standing on this remote landscape jutting into Lake Superior. The original site boasted a keeper's house, fog signal and several other structures. It is doubtful that the tower will survive despite the sandbagging efforts of the Luce County community.

Old Point Loma Lighthouse
San Diego, California

Guiding ships into San Diego Harbor since 1855, Old Point Loma Lighthouse is one of the first eight lighthouses built on the West Coast. A cylindrical brick tower rises from the center of a stone, Cape Cod-style dwelling. Out of service since 1891, the lighthouse was almost demolished. Restored by the National Park Service in 1935, Old Point Loma Lighthouse is now a part of the Cabrillo National Monument.

Sitka Lighthouse
Sitka, Alaska

The first American light placed on the Alaskan coast was an unnamed beacon light established at Sitka in 1895. Increased shipping traffic and several shipwrecks along the rocky shores of Sitka Sound prompted Congress, in 1900, to place additional aides to navigation on the southeast and west coasts of Alaska. This light is located on Cape Edgecumbe.

Point Montara Light
Pacifica, California

Three decades passed and many ships ran aground and wrecked before the fog signal at Point Montara became a light station in 1900. Just south of San Francisco and north of Half Moon Bay, the 30-foot conical tower has an automated light with a focal plane 70 feet above sea level — and the fog signal is gone. Most of the buildings are now used as a youth hostel.

Bodie Island Light
Oregon Inlet, North Carolina

The third lighthouse to be built on the site, Bodie Island Light guided ships through the perilous Oregon Inlet. Beginning service in 1872, the 163-foot conical tower is painted with wide black and white horizontal bands. A heavy wire netting covers the lantern to prevent flocks of birds from damaging the lens. Now a part of Cape Hatteras National Seashore, the keeper's quarters house a visitors center and museum.

Pemaquid Point Light
Pemaquid Point, Maine

At the entrance to the calm waters of St. John's Bay stands the picturesque rubblestone 38-foot tower of Pemaquid Point Light. Pemaquid Point was the site of one of the worst shipwrecks in Maine history when in 1903 the schooner George Edmunds ran off course and struck the rocks just west of the lighthouse. Sitting on a high cliff, the dwelling was replaced in 1857 and still stands today — now housing the Fisherman's Museum.

angara Lighthouse
ngara Island, Inside Passage, Canada

ommissioned in 1913, Langara, in the Queen Charlottes, is one of the most isolated ghthouses in Canada. Located on Langara Island on the northern end of the Inside ssage, the reinforced concrete tower, fortified with six buttresses, is fitted with a st order lens to direct vessels toward Prince Rupert.

Fanad Head Light
Northern coast of Ireland

Facing the North Atlantic, the
Fanad Head Light has been
guiding ships in and out of
Lough Swilly southwest of
Inishtrahull since 1817.

Peggy's Cove Lighthouse
Nova Scotia, Canada

Big Sable Point Lighthouse
Ludington State Park, Michigan

Originally built in 1867 to guide ships along the eastern shore of Lake Michigan, Big Sable Point Lighthouse began to deteriorate in the early 1900s. The 107-foot conical brick tower was encased in steel and reinforced with concrete. Its location in Ludington State Park and its broad black middle stripe make Big Sable one of the most scenic and easily recognizable lighthouses in the United States.

Grand Haven South Pierhead Inner Light and the Grand Haven South Pierhead Light
Grand Haven, Michigan

Ships sailing into shipping lanes farther into Lake Michigan are guided by the red lights of the Grand Haven South Pierhead Inner Light and the Grand Haven South Pierhead Light. The Inner Light is a 51-foot red steel conical tower. The iron-clad South Pierhead Light was originally the fog signal building. It was moved to the end of the public pier in 1905.

Previous page:
Portland Head Lighthouse
South Portland, Maine

West Quoddy Head Lighthouse
Lubec, Maine

One of Maine's most picturesque lighthouses, painted with red and white candy-striped bands, West Quoddy Lighthouse stands on a cliff on the easternmost point in the United States. The first lighthouse in the United States to use a fog bell, the keeper would receive an additional sixty dollars each year to strike the bell by hand. Guiding ships around Campobello Island and the dangerous waters of the Bay of Fundy, the present 49-foot tower was built in 1858 to replace the original 1808 station.

Highlands (Cape Cod) Lighthouse
Truro, Massachusetts

Cape Cod Light, built in 1798 on the highlands near Truro, was the first lighthouse on Cape Cod. Aiding sailors bound from Europe to the Massachusetts Bay, it served as a beacon between Nantucket and Cape Ann. The 66-foot tower and adjoining buildings are currently threatened by erosion.

Marshall Point Lighthouse
Port Clyde, Maine

Marshall Point Lighthouse is built on a boulder outcrop located at the entrance to Port Clyde Harbor. A wooden bridge connects the white conical tower to the land. The keeper's dwelling and surviving oil house are maintained by the St. George Historical Society.

Fond du Lac Range Front Light
Fond du Lac, Wisconsin

Maintained by the city of Fond du Lac as a private aid to navigation, Fond du Lac Range Front Light was established in 1943. Located on the west side of the entrance to the Fond du Lac Yacht Basin's Lakeridge Park, its focal plane is 60 feet tall and the light's range is 14 miles.

Au Sable Point Light
Grand Marais, Michigan

To light the dangerous coast between Whitefish Point & Grand Island Harbor Au Sable Point light was built in 1874. Strewn with shipwrecks, the treacherous dark stretch of shoreline was known as the "Graveyard Coast." One of the most remote mainland light stations in America, keepers could reach the station only by boat or wagon, followed by a three-mile hike. The Coast Guard automated the 87-foot brick tower in 1958 and today it maintains a solar-powered light mounted on the lighthouse catwalk. The keeper's house and property are part of Pictured Rocks National Lakeshore.

die Island Light
gon Inlet, North Carolina

e third lighthouse to be built on the site, Bodie Island ht guided ships through the perilous Oregon Inlet. ginning service in 1872, the 163-foot conical tower is nted with wide black and white horizontal bands. A vy wire netting covers the lantern to prevent flocks of ds from damaging the lens. Now a part of Cape Hatteras tional Seashore, the keeper's quarters house a visitors ter and museum.

Trinidad Head Lighthouse
Trinidad, California

Established on Cape Mendocino in 1871, this 25-foot lighthouse on a small brick tower serves ships traveling close to shore. A foghorn has replaced the fog bell, which now stands beside the lighthouse.

Sherwood Point
Door County, Wisconsin

The last manned lighthouse on the Great Lakes, Sherwood Point Lighthouse, built in
1883 and not automated until 1983, marks the entrance to Sturgeon Bay. It is the
only Door County lighthouse built with red brick, not limestone or cream-colored
brick. The ten-sided cast iron lantern sits atop a 35-foot square tower with an
attached two-story dwelling.

Tawas Point Li(
Tawas City, Michi

By the 1870s, the shoreline of Lake Huron had built up so much that the Ta
Point Lighthouse on the north side of the entrance to Saginaw Bay stood m
than one mile from the lake. In 1876, a 68-foot conical white tower connected t
one-and-a-half-story red brick keeper's dwelling, replaced the original lighthou

Point Wilson Lighthouse
Port Townsend, Washington

To serve as an additional guide into Admiralty Inlet, a light was established on the western shore in 1879. A fog signal was placed in an adjacent building to assist ships that may become lost in the fog. Beach erosion threatened the light by 1904 and rock was piled up to save the lighthouse. A new 46-foot octagonal tower of reinforced concrete was put into service by 1914 and is still active today.

endota (Bete Grise) Light
ndota Heights, Minnesota

ow privately owned, the square yellow brick tower ached to the eastern end of a two-story keeper's dwelling opped by a 10-sided cast iron lantern. Built in 1895, it laced the first wooden tower which guided ships into Mendota Ship Canal linking Lac La Belle with Lake perior. With new Pierhead lights placed in 1960 at the trance to Lac La Belle, the Coast Guard decommissioned te Grise.

Grosse Point Light
Evanston, Illinois

Serving as a primary coastal light for Lake Michigan, Grosse Point Light's second order Fresnel lens is one of the most powerful on the lakes. The beautiful 110-foot conical tower is painted yellow and trimmed in red. Built in 1873, along with a two-story double keeper's dwelling and two other brick structures used as storage barns, the deteriorating brick tower was encased in concrete in 1914. Now located adjacent to Northwestern University, the tower is used as a private aid to navigation and the buildings are used as a nature center and maritime museum open to the public on weekends.

Point Cabrillo Lighthouse
near Mendocino, California

The quaint wooden Cape Cod style of Point Cabrillo lighthouse is typical of California's earliest lighthouses. Lit in 1909, the 47-foot tall tower, rising from the fog signal building, is the only lighthouse between Point Arena and Cape Mendocino. Its location near a town, fertile land for gardens and livestock, and spacious, comfortable dwellings made Point Cabrillo a popular station with keepers. The light was automated in the 1970s.

Barnegat Light, "Old Barney"
Long Beach Island, New Jersey

Forty-five miles south of Sandy Hook at the north end of Long Beach Island stands "Old Barney." Built in 1858, the new 161-foot tall tower replaced the inadequate, poorly constructed 1835 light. Initiation of the Barnegat Lightship in 1927 fulfilled the tower's function and Old Barney was retired in 1944.

Holland Harbor South Pierhead Light ("Big Red")
Holland Harbor, Michigan

The wooden light station built in 1872 was replaced in 1907 with a keeper's quarters and steel skeleton light tower. In 1936, the light was placed in one of the twin gables of the keeper's quarters. Encased in steel plates to protect it from heavy poundings during storms of Lake Michigan, the Holland Harbor South Pierhead Light is painted red with a black slate, gabled roof.

Hunting Island Lighthou
Beaufort, South Caro

It remains a mystery as to the fate of the original lighthouse built on Hunt Island in 1859. No longer standing after the Civil War, a new 95-foot cast-i tower lined with bricks was built about one mile away along with a thr story keeper's house and several outbuildings. The voracious seas proved hungry for the structures so in 1889 the tower was disassembled and reb one and one quarter miles inland. The light is no longer act

Point Judith Light
Point Judith, Rhode Island

Saving sailors from eternal rest at the bottom of the "graveyard of the Atlantic,"
Point Judith Light was built on the point marking the entrance to Narragansett
Bay in 1810. This meek wooden structure blown over by gale winds in 1815 was
replaced by a stone tower the next year. The current Point Judith Lighthouse, built
in 1857, is an octagonal granite block 65-foot tower. With the upper half painted
brown and the lower half white, it appears as a strikingly handsome day mark.

South Breakwater Outer Lighthouse
Duluth, Minnesota

A pair of light towers were built in 1901 on a pier
beside the channel connecting the inner harbor to Lake
Superior. This Outer Lighthouse is a 35-foot tower
built on the corner of a brick fog signal building.

Crooked River Lighthouse
Carrabelle, Florida

The Crooked River Lighthouse, its upper half painted dark red and lower half painted white, was commissioned in 1889 to replace the Dog Island Light Station, which was swept into the sea in the an 1873 storm. The 115-foot tower's fourth order lens guides lumber boats and freighters into the deep entrance of the Crooked River.

Boca Grande Rear Range Light
Gasparilla Island, Florida

Boca Grande Rear Range Light, located one mile from
the southern tip of Gasparilla Island, was built in 1932 to
replace local beacons fueled by whale oil. The electric red
light, supported by a white hexagonal skeletal tower,
guides vessels into the Port Boca Grande Yacht Basin.

. Augustine Lighthouse
Augustine, Florida

Whitefish Point Light
Whitefish Point, Michigan

Cape Florida Lighthou
Key Biscayne, Flor

Cape Florida Lighthouse, located on Cape Florida at the northern entrance
Biscayne Bay, was built in 1825. Florida's oldest lighthouse was attacked
Seminole Indians in 1836 and put out of service until 1846. The light was ag
damaged during the Civil War and restored in 1866. Serving as a daymark sir
1878 when a new light was built on Fowey Rocks, Cape Florida Lightho
was recommissioned by the Coast Guard and relit 100 years la

Forty Mile Point Light
Rogers City, Michigan

Forty Mile Point Light was placed in operation in 1897 to light a dark and dangerous gap in the 50 mile coastline between Presque Isle and Cheboygan on Lake Huron. The white painted square brick tower stands 53 feet tall attached to a red brick keeper's dwelling. Forty Mile Point is well maintained and flashes a white light from its fourth order lens 66 feet above lake level. Now a part of Presque Isle County Park, the light station also has a brick oil house, a fog signal building and two brick privies.

arblehead Lighthouse
y Point, Ohio

ie oldest active lighthouse on the Great Lakes erlooks the entrance to Sandusky Bay at Bay Point. t on a solid stone beach, the conical stone tower, iginally 55 feet tall, was raised to 65 feet late in the ieteenth century. Guiding sailors home from Lake ie, the light was also visible to Confederate soldiers ld as prisoners of war on nearby Johnson's Island.

Algoma North Pierhead Light
Algoma, Wisconsin

At the end of the pier at the mouth of the Ahnapee River stands the round, red metal tower of the Algoma North Pierhead Light. First constructed in 1893 and rebuilt in 1908, the smaller tapered top level of the lighthouse was raised to a height of 42 feet by adding a new steel base in 1932.

Cheboygan Crib Light
Cheboygan, Michigan

The Cheboygan Crib Lighthouse guided sailors from Lake Michigan into the Cheboygan River. A crumbling foundation consisting of concrete and stone caused the lighthouse to fall into the channel of the Cheboygan River. Residents rescued the drowning lighthouse and placed it in a park at the end of a short pier.

Split Rock Lighthouse
Two Harbors, Minnesota

In 1910, high on a cliff above Lake Superior, the difficult task of building the Split Rock Lighthouse was completed. Once helping ore-carrying vessels to navigate the severe winter Lake Superior storms, the octagonal yellow brick tower was decommissioned in 1969. Along with three dwellings, a fog signal building, an oil house, and other barns and outbuildings, the lighthouse is now a part of Split Rock State Park.

Cape Florida Lighthouse
Key Biscayne, Florida

Lighthouse keeper's house
Año Nuevo State Reserve, San Mateo County, California

nitowoc Breakwater Light
e Michigan, Wisconsin

e present structure of the Manitowoc Breakwater Light and steel-plated fog signal
isc were completed in 1918 at the mouth of the Manitowoc River. It rests on a
icrete pier on a concrete breakwall. The watchroom is 40 feet high, fitted with a
i order lens. Its focal plane is 51 feet above lake level.

Nobska Point Light
Falmouth, Massachusetts

The Nobska Point Light warns sailors away from two dangerous shoals called Hedge Fence and L'Hommedieu in Woods Hole off the southwest tip of Cape Cod with its fourth order lens guarding the junction of Nantucket Sound and Vineyard Sound. The iron-shelled, brick-lined tower, built in 1876, stands 42 feet tall with a focal plane 87 feet above sea level.

waunee Pier Light
aunee, Wisconsin

e square white tower of the Kewaunee Pierhead Light was built on top of the ginal fog signal building in 1931. Previously, a pair of range lights was located on Lake Michigan pier.

Big Bay Point Light
Big Bay, Michigan

The square red brick tower, white watch room, and two-story red brick keeper's quarters were built in 1896 to light a dark stretch of the Upper Peninsula Lake Superior coast. The light was automated in 1941, decommissioned in 1961, and in 1986 its private owner converted Big Bay Point Light into a bed-and-breakfast inn.

Pigeon Point Lighthouse
Pescadero, California

On the coastal highway between San Francisco and Santa Cruz, the picturesque New England-style Pigeon Point Lighthouse protects ships from the dangerous shoals off California's rocky shoreline. Completed in 1872, Pigeon Point Lighthouse, named for the shipwrecked "Carrier Pigeon," is a 115-foot-tall brick circular structure. Today the light is automated and the station serves as a youth hostel.

Quaco Lightstation
St. Martins, New Brunswick

Pigeon Point Lighthouse
Pescadero, California

Smalls Lighthouse
Smalls, Irish Sea, twenty miles from the Welsh mainland

e British Isles are noted for offshore lighthouses and the engineers who built
m. John Phillips obtained the lease for a low rock outcropping in the Irish Sea.
swering an advertisement for a lighthouse design was Henry Whiteside, who
igned a simple wooden structure to be assembled ashore, then disassembled and
nsported to its site. By the end of 1776, the lighthouse was lit. Stormy seas caused
nage to the supports and Trinity House took over repairs, putting Smalls back into
vice in 1778. Weathering storms until 1861, Smalls was replaced by a 107-foot
ne lighthouse built by James Douglas.

Waugoshance Shoal Light
Northwest of Wisland, Michigan

Warning ships of the shallow depths of the
Straits of Mackinac, the Waugoshance Shoal
Light was built in 1851. Decommissioned in
1912, this structure is barely standing today.

oquille River Light
ndon, Oregon

aptains of lumber carrying vessels navigating the Coquille
iver at the end of the nineteenth century demanded a
ht at the river's treacherous entrance. First lit in 1896, the
-foot stucco-coated brick tower light burned for forty
ars. Replaced by a series of buoys and a small jetty light, it
mained empty and inactive longer than it was in use. In
e 1970s the state of Oregon rescued the lighthouse and
maining properties from destructive vandals, restored them
d made them part of Bullard Beach State Park.

Plate on light, West San Benito Island, Baja California

Remains of clock work mechanism,
West San Benito Island, Baja California

Port Dalhousie
Front Range Light
Port Dalhousie, Ontario, Canada

The white octagonal tower of Port Dalhousie Front Range Light stands at the entrance to Port Dalhousie Harbor on Lake Ontario. Two other lights had been built on this site in 1852 and 1893 but were destroyed by foul weather and lightning.

Holland Harbor South
Pierhead Lighthouse
Holland Harbor, Michigan

Longships Lighthouse
Cornwall, England

In 1795, Lieutenant Henry Smith began building the Longships Lighthouse to protect ships from the threatening cliffs of Land's End and the quick-forming fog banks. Trinity House took over completion of Longships in 1836 when Smith went bankrupt. Rough seas often washed over the lantern until a taller, 117-foot tower was built in 1883. A helicopter pad constructed over the lantern is a very prominent feature.

bbs Hill Lighthouse
nuda, West Indies

s 130-foot tower of brick, concrete, and cast-iron
es was built in England and transported to the island
Bermuda. A spiral staircase connects seven floors until
aches the interior of the lamp room.

Fort Jefferson Lighthouse
Dry Tortugas, Florida

Construction began on Fort Jefferson, the largest masonry fort in the United States, in 1846 around the original 1825 light house at Dry Tortugas. In 1876, a new Fort Jefferson Light was placed at the top of a staircase in the fort's walls. The 37-foot tall iron-plated hexagonal tower guided ships sailing to and from the Gulf of Mexico. The fort was closed in 1912 and the light deactivated.

Sodus Point Light
Lake Ontario, New York

Originally built in 1825 on a bluff just west of the bay entrance on Lake Ontario, the lighthouse was rebuilt for the last time in 1871. The 45-foot limestone tower and attached two-story dwelling, decommissioned in 1901, currently house a maritime museum.

Heceta Head Lighthouse
Near Florence, Oregon

To light the dark stretch of coast between Cape Foulweather and Cape Arago, Heceta Head Lighthouse was lit in 1894. The 56-foot conical masonry tower and several outbuildings stand on the rocky Oregon coast surrounded by the picturesque scenery of Siuslaw National Forest.

olf Rock Lighthouse
Lands End, coast of Cornwall, England

nstruction of the Wolf Rock Lighthouse began in 1862, ith the last stone laid in 1869. This granite tower was ghted for the first time in 1870. A landing boat is used to change light keepers who are sometimes hauled back the boat through the surf.

Eagle Harbor Lighthouse
Eagle Harbor, Michigan

Santa Cruz Light
Lighthouse Point,
Santa Cruz, California

111